CREATURE CAMOUFLAGE

HIDING IN RAIN FORESTS

Deborah Underwood

Heinemann Library
Chicago, Illinois

www.heinemannraintree.com
Visit our website to find out more information about Heinemann-Raintree books.

To order:
 Phone 888-454-2279
Visit www.heinemannraintree.com to browse our catalog and order online.

© 2011 Heinemann Library
an imprint of Capstone Global Library, LLC
Chicago, Illinois

All rights reserved. No part of this publication may be reproduced or transmitted in any form or by any means, electronic or mechanical, including photocopying, recording, taping, or any information storage and retrieval system, without permission in writing from the publisher.

Edited by Rebecca Rissman and Nancy Dickmann
Designed by Joanna Hinton Malivoire
Picture research by Tracy Cummins
Originated by Capstone Global Library
Printed and bound in China by Leo Paper Products Ltd

15 14 13 12 11
10 9 8 7 6 5 4 3 2 1

Library of Congress Cataloging-in-Publication Data
Underwood, Deborah.
  Hiding in rain forests / Deborah Underwood. -- 1st ed.
      p. cm. -- (Creature camouflage)
  Includes bibliographical references and index.
  ISBN 978-1-4329-4026-3 (hc) -- ISBN 978-1-4329-4035-5 (pb) 1. Rain forest animals--Juvenile literature. 2. Camouflage (Biology)--Juvenile literature. I. Title.
  QL112.U535 2011
  591.47'2--dc22
                                                       2009051775

Acknowledgments
The author and publisher are grateful to the following for permission to reproduce copyright material: FLPA pp. 23, 24 (Chris Mattison); Getty Images pp. 7 (Panoramic Images) 13, 14, 29 (George Grall), 27 (Connie Coleman); Minden Pictures pp. 11, 12 (Norbert Wu); National Geographic Stock pp. 8 (Minden Pictures/Michael Patricia Fogden), 25, 26 (Minden Pictures/Mitsuhiko Imamori), 28 (Minden Pictures/Konrad Wothe); naturepl.com pp. 9, 17, 18, 19, 20 (© Pete Oxford), 15, 16 (© Nick Garbutt), 21, 22 (© Francois Savigny); Photolibrary p. 10 (John Warburton-Lee Photography); Shutterstock pp. 4 (© Map Resources), 5 (© Dr. Morley Read), 6 (© cameilia).

Cover image of a warty green burrowing frog (Scaphiophryne marmorata) camouflaged, in Madagascar, is used with permission of Naturepl.com (Edwin Giesbers).

We would like to thank Michael Bright for his invaluable help in the preparation of this book.

Every effort has been made to contact copyright holders of any material reproduced in this book. Any omissions will be rectified in subsequent printings if notice is given to the publisher.

All the Internet addresses (URLs) given in this book were valid at the time of going to press. However, due to the dynamic nature of the Internet, some addresses may have changed, or sites may have changed or ceased to exist since publication. While the author and publisher regret any inconvenience this may cause readers, no responsibility for any such changes can be accepted by either the author or the publisher.

Contents

What Are Rain Forests Like?........ 4

Living in a Rain Forest............. 6

What Is Camouflage?............. 8

Find the Rain Forest Animals........11

Animals that Stand Out 28

Glossary........................ *30*

Find Out More................... *31*

Index........................... *32*

Some words are printed in bold, **like this**. You can find out what they mean by looking in the glossary.

What Are Rain Forests Like?

Forests are places where trees are the main kind of plant. A rain forest is a forest that gets lots of rain. Some rain forests are warm and some are cool.

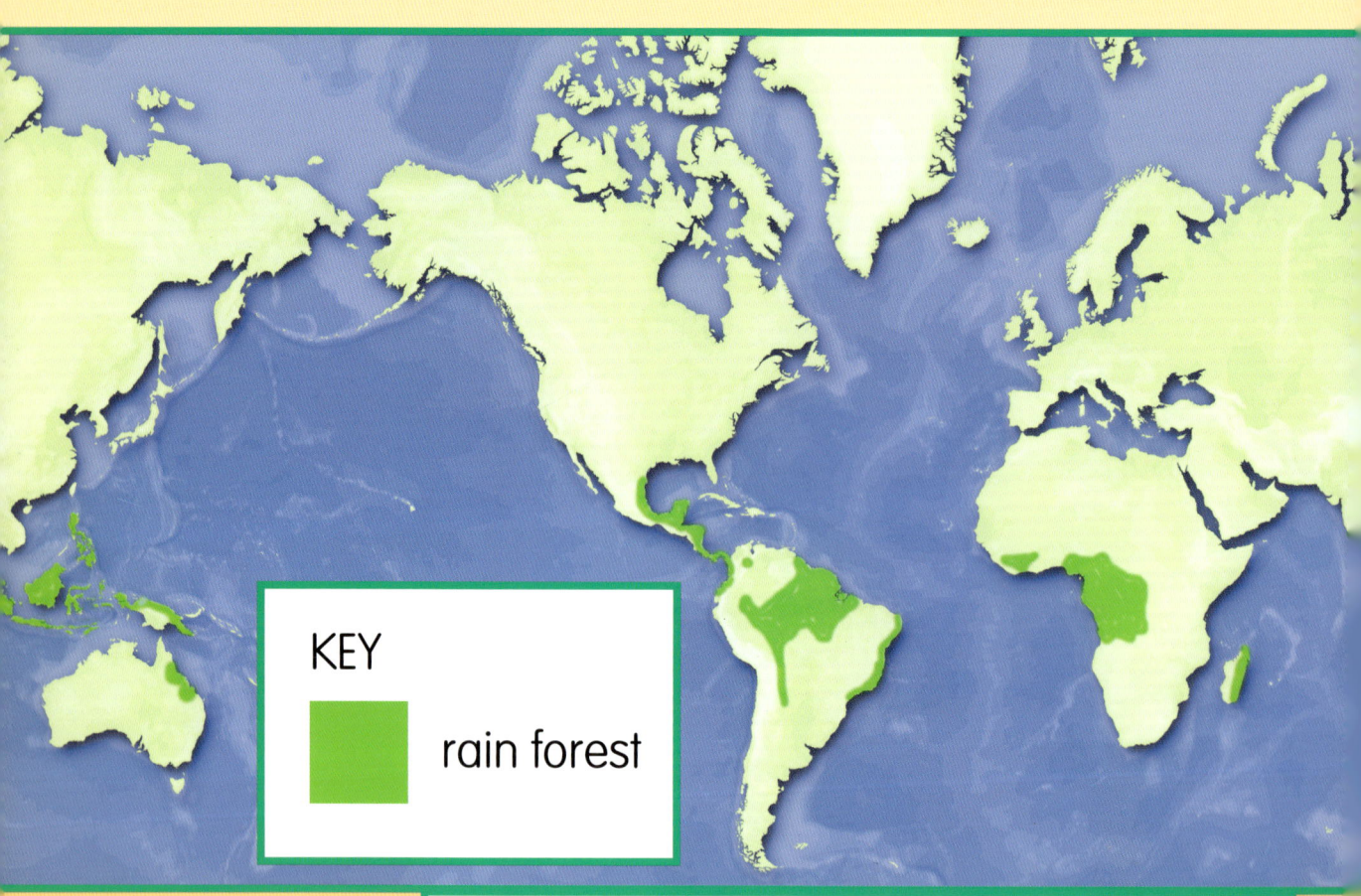

Tropical rain forests are found in places where the weather is always warm.

Rain forests are thick forests with tall trees and many other plants.

The animals in this book live in **tropical** rain forests. Tropical rain forests are warm all year round. Rain forests are full of food—so they are full of life!

Living in a Rain Forest

Monkeys, parrots, and many other animals live in rain forests. Some live high in the trees. Others live on the ground. All rain forest animals must **survive** in a hot, wet **environment**.

Lemurs spend most of their time up in the trees.

This butterfly's wings are brown underneath. Lifting up its wings can help it hide from birds.

Rain forest animals have special **features** that help them survive in their surroundings. These features are called **adaptations**.

What Is Camouflage?

Camouflage (KAM-uh-flaj) is an **adaptation** that helps animals hide. The color of an animal's skin, fur, or feathers may match the things around it.

A jaguar's spots help it hide in the rain forest.

Caimans are related to alligators. This caiman looks like part of a log!

Animals that eat other animals are called **predators**. Camouflage makes it easier for them to hide. This helps them catch food.

Animals that **predators** eat are called **prey** animals. **Camouflage** helps them, too. A prey animal hides so it will not become a predator's meal!

What makes this chameleon (kuh-MEE-lee-uhn) blend in with the leaves?

Find the Rain Forest Animals

Three-toed sloth

Some kinds of three-toed sloths (slawths) live high in rain forest trees. Can you see how the color of their fur helps them **blend in**?

CAMOUFLAGED

Sloths move very slowly. They cannot run from danger. Their fur helps them hide from **predators**, such as jaguars.

Leaf katydid

When is a leaf not a leaf? When it is a leaf katydid (KAY-tee-did)! Animals such as bats, birds, lizards, and spiders eat katydids. A leaf katydid's colors help it hide from them.

CAMOUFLAGED

REVEALED

Some katydids are green, like leaves. Some are brown, like tree **bark**. They are active at night. During the day, katydids hold very still so they are hard to spot.

Horned frog

Horned frogs live on the forest floor. They have two points on their heads. The frogs' colors and shape make them look like dead leaves.

CAMOUFLAGED

Horned frogs use **camouflage** when they catch food. A frog holds very still until **prey** passes by. Then the frog shoots out a sticky tongue and gobbles up the prey!

CAMOUFLAGED

Leaf-tailed gecko

A leaf-tailed gecko (GECK-oh) can flatten its body against a tree. Its tail is shaped like a leaf. This lets the gecko hide while it sleeps.

The tail helps the gecko in another way, too. If a **predator** grabs a gecko's tail, the tail drops off. This lets the gecko escape! Then the gecko grows a new tail.

REVEALED

CAMOUFLAGED

Imperial moth

The imperial (im-PEER-ee-uhl) moth has a good way of hiding in a rain forest. It looks like a leaf! When it holds still, it disappears among the leaves on the forest floor.

An imperial moth does not eat when it is an adult. Other animals might try to eat it, though! The moth's shape and color help keep hungry animals from spotting it.

CAMOUFLAGED

Great potoo

Potoo (POH-too) birds hunt at night and sleep during the day. Potoos have feathers that look like tree **bark**. This helps sleeping birds stay safe.

REVEALED

If danger comes near, potoos close their eyes. They point their beaks up to the sky. This makes the potoos look even more like tree branches!

Reticulated python

Reticulated pythons (reh-TIH-kyoo-lay-tuhd PY-thonz) are the world's longest snakes. They can be over 30 feet long! Can you see how its skin **pattern** helps the snake **blend in**?

CAMOUFLAGED

REVEALED

Sometimes a python hunts by hiding in a tree. Its **camouflage** helps it hide. When **prey** passes below, the python catches it. Then it swallows the prey whole.

Orchid mantis

The orchid mantis (OR-kihd MAN-tis) looks like a flower! Its legs are shaped like petals. It is very hard to spot a mantis on a plant.

CAMOUFLAGED

The orchid mantis eats other insects. It sits and waits until **prey** comes by. Then the mantis grabs the prey with its front legs.

This owl monkey's fur helps it hide in rain forest trees.

The rain forest is full of animals with **camouflage**. If you are ever lucky enough to visit a rain forest, look closely. You never know what you might see!

Animals that Stand Out

Some kinds of birds of paradise live on the island of New Guinea. There are few large **predators** on the island. So the birds do not need to hide.

Male birds of paradise have bright colors that help them attract mates.

The blue poison arrow frog stands out in the rain forest.

Poison arrow frogs have **poisons** in their skins. Their bright colors warn predators not to eat them. The frogs come in many colors. One kind is red with blue legs. It is called a blue jeans frog!

Glossary

adaptation special feature that helps an animal survive in its surroundings

bark tough, outer part of a tree trunk

blend in matches well with the things around it

camouflage adaptation that helps an animal blend in

environment place where an animal lives

feature special part of an animal

pattern shapes and marks on an animals skin, fur, or feathers

poison something dangerous that can make you sick, or even kill you

predator animal that eats other animals

prey animal that other animals eat

survive stay alive

tropical place that is very warm all year round

Find Out More

Books to read

Berkes, Marianne, and Jeanette Canyon (illustrator). *Over in the Jungle: A Rainforest Rhyme.* Nevada City, CA: Dawn Publications, 2007.

Mitchell, Susan K., and Connie McLennan (illustrator). *The Rainforest Grew All Around.* Mount Pleasant, SC: Sylvan Dell Publishing, 2007.

Websites

www.mbgnet.net/sets/rforest/
Tropical rain forest animal information from the Missouri Botanical Garden.

www.rainforest-alliance.org/resources.cfm?id=facts
Facts from the Rain Forest Alliance.

Index

adaptations 7, 8

birds 13, 21–22, 28
birds of paradise 28
blending 8, 9, 10, 11, 12, 13, 14, 17, 19, 20, 22, 23, 24, 25
blue jeans frogs 29

cold 4
color 8, 11, 13, 14, 15, 20, 29

feathers 8, 21
frogs 15–16, 29
fur 8, 11, 12

heat 4, 5, 6
horned frogs 15–16

imperial moths 19–20
insects 13–14, 19–20, 25–26

leaf katydids 13–14
leaf-tailed geckos 17–18
leaves 13, 14, 15, 17, 19

monkeys 6

orchid mantises 25–26

parrots 6
patterns 23
poison arrow frogs 29
potoo birds 21–22
predators 9, 10, 12, 15–16, 18, 21, 23–24, 25–26, 28, 29
prey 10, 11–12, 13–14, 16, 17–18, 19–20, 21–22, 24, 26, 28, 29

rain 4, 6
reptiles 17–18, 23–24
reticulated pythons 23–24

shapes 15, 17, 20, 25
skin 8, 23, 29
standing out 28–29

tails 17–18
three-toed sloths 11–12
trees 4, 6, 11, 14, 17, 21, 22, 24
tropical rain forests 5